A Poetic Guide to the Most Powerful Forces on Earth

A. Brailow

BookLeaf Publishing

India | USA | UK

Presentation by *BookLeaf Publishing*

Web: www.bookleafpub.com

E-mail: info@bookleafpub.com

ISBN: 9789358318128

First edition 2023

PREFACE

When the prince spoke those words, after some time had passed, the young girl who would become a princess was at once delighted, confused, and worried. It wasn't the proposal. He was the first person who had asked in a world that proved, time and time again, that it wasn't made for her. In this lovely place with gradients of green fields and perfect blossoms to live in, though not so perfect as to seem artificial, there was no question that she wanted to stay. She did want to stay with him.

He wanted to call her Maya.

She was no longer the size of anyone's thumb in this place, so she supposed it would be appropriate to take another name, but Thumbelina was still feeling unsure. Something about it bothered her.

"Wait…" Her voice trembled.

The prince's mouth opened slightly, and his brows furrowed in concern.

"No, no, it's okay," Thumbelina reassured him. "I just want to speak with my dear swallow first. He's always been my friend and companion. I'm very grateful for everything that he's done for me, and I'm also grateful that you let me into your home and your heart. I promise that I care deeply for you. I've also been through a lot, and he's been my first confidant at the most difficult of times. In those depths, he brought me to you, so please understand."

"Of course." The prince still looked worried, but his expression had softened to what felt like concern for her rather than concern his feelings would be reciprocated.

The swallow wasn't far away, but he would soon return to the old forest. He had known that the prince was going to propose to Thumbelina, and he knew that he had done the right thing by bringing her away from that mole. It was instinctual. He had to take her away from there. More than once, she had saved his life.

"Swallow! Swallow!" Thumbelina called out, running towards him clumsily.

"Thumbelina! I thought you were with the prince. Did things not go well?" The swallow tilted his head slightly.

"No, that's not it. He's asked me to marry him, and I want to—"

"Oh, well, that's wonderful! Thank goodness you never married that mole!"

"Yes, but—"

"What's wrong, Thumbelina? Do you feel it's too sudden?"

"Swallow, it's not the marriage, it's my name. He wants to call me Maya. I think I understand what he's trying to do, but my name was the first gift I ever received from my mother aside from that pretty dress she made me. You remember what happened to that."

The swallow nodded gravely, signing that she should continue.

"I spent so much time trying to get back home for a reason, and I think she might have lost hope of me coming back by now. I want to somehow let her know I'm okay. At least, I wish

I could. At the same time, I don't want to lose the only thing I have left to tie me to her."

The swallow thought carefully about his friend's answer. In all the time he had spent with her, he had spent so much time keeping her safe from harm, or at least trying to in all the ways he knew how, that Thumbelina's mother had hardly ever crossed his mind excepting the few times she'd tell stories about her. Silently, he cursed himself for not paying more attention. Taking Thumbelina to her mother wouldn't be too difficult for him, but the moment called him back again. That would only solve one of her problems.

"Thumbelina…you're right that names are a gift. When they are given, they become your own. They have the meaning that you give to them. Your name is your own, and if Thumbelina is who you are, then that is who you will be. You can keep it or change it as you see fit, but you will always be you, and you will always be my best friend. As long as I have been coming back and forth between the forest and this place, I have gotten to know the prince as well. I think that he believes naming you again would help you. He has heard of your pain, and maybe he wanted to rename you in order to help you start a new life away from that pain. As your friend, I know it wasn't always painful for you, that there are times you treasure. It's okay if you need him to understand that. There is nothing wrong with who you are or how you feel, and I am so happy that you are in my life. I'm not the only one who thinks so. Didn't your mother tell you that you should want to be exactly who you are?"

Thumbelina was listening carefully, her head resting on the swallow's chest.

"Mhm," she spoke in a low, tired voice. "She did. It feels like so much longer ago."

The two of them sat together, just thinking in comfortable silence. A half an hour passed, and they watched dandelion seeds blow in the wind. Thumbelina smiled and reached up as if they would brush her palm.

"What do you want to do, Thumbelina?"

She smiled at that question. Again, he was one of very few in her life who had ever asked her that or something like it.

"I think I want to wait. I think, if I decide that I want a new name, I will rename myself. If you say the prince will understand, I believe you, but I'll talk to him about it."

"I'm sure he will. Thumbelina?"

"Yes, dear Swallow?"

"Would you…like me to go and speak to your mother for you? Maybe I'll take you to her?"

"I would like that very much. Could you?"

"Of course, and Thumbelina?"

She looked up expectantly.

"Being yourself is the best thing you can be. It's a powerful thing to be yourself."

Thumbelina closed her eyes and smiled to herself.

"Thank you, Swallow. I needed that."

A Defeat Better Than Many Victories

Surrender had been
the greatest of failings
until you are assured you are
someone worth saving.
Then, to surrender is to save oneself.

To be assured that you are
someone worth saving,
you might fall backward,
and chasing the sunlight,
someone will catch you
in time.

Surrender, but to whom?
Happiness,
found in the net of words
that caught you
when you fell backward.
Surrender to this.
If anything,
surrender to this.

Surrender, but to whom?
Innocence,

that scatters dandelion seeds
with its breath
and thought it was sweet.
Surrender to this,
if nothing else.

Surrender, but to whom?
Understanding,
even if it isn't understood
especially if what isn't understood
encompasses who sits beside you.
Surrender to this.
If anything,
surrender to this.

The Brightest Sense You've Ever Known

The steel beam begins to rise
as footsteps cross
and the rope is pulled,
and you float.

The steel beam rises
and you float
on the dust
that circles your fingertips.

Resting on that golden glow,
peace,
and the brightest sense
you've ever known.

The Most Brilliant Capture

It's that feeling when
somebody tells you
to close your eyes
and you feel a softness surround you,
drawing you back,
coloring inside and outside
your lines,
and your fingers move expertly
through the clouds,
eyes still closed,
and captured in a daydream.

Know me and find me
in these clouds.
Find your feet or
fall through,
indisposed to the story.

Allow my surrender.
That was worth everything.

It's that feeling when
the sounds that surround you
cannot be described.
They can only be touched

as the bird with the green wing
touches the shallow pool,
asking for nothing.

That familiar softness
sharpens with the wind,
and you accept the
carefully crafted warmth,
a calloused warmth.

Give it light,
enough to see by,
and you feel like
something of a blank slate
ready to, happily, give in again.

The artist knows what that means.
You point to what you understand,
and she fills in the spaces.
At your sign,
she colors inside and outside
your lines.
Your fingers move expertly
through the clouds,
and you give more.

Left Behind

You don't think you'll ever see a lot of things,
like a civilization left behind that there are only
imaginings of, until you see it. At some point,
you've thought about what that's meant or read
about it, but feeling it is an entirely different
experience.

In among the stones
you don't know why
you want them to stay
and to keep all they've left,
but you do
if for no other reason
than it feels right.

You don't stop to wonder why you're there, and
when a figure emerges, the only other signal of
life in the way you've always understood life,
they've heard you. They've heard your music,
and inasmuch as you revere this remnant of a
world you could never know, every note betrays
your inability to exist within these bounds.

Anything but yourself,
someone completely different,

and at first,
that search is for personas.

Personas can be left.
They are the masks,
free to remove.
Someone completely different
that asks for more.

Someone completely different
means there's a hidden world,
a lost civilization,
began,
but never filled.

The figure takes you on their ship, and they
know the face you wear does not fit the voice
they heard. On the ship, your face can match
your name as nothing else ever could.

Someone lives here,
not alone,
but someone lives here.
No one else ever could,
not to stay.
They built the stones up,
and left them there.

When they burned,

they needed you,
your music,
your face.

The Shape of the World

Though diamonds were plentiful,
there was one,
and it was chosen.
It changed little,
though the means for its existence
changed the world
and its outcomes.

Diamonds are plentiful,
which is why
we discard them,
and we understand
far too much of them.

This imperceptible past
yields the understanding
that no diamond but
this one,
and no face but
this one,
and none but
this
will hold the shape
of my desires.

Deep Gratitude

I told myself that I
would not write today
and someone was
behind me,
beside me,
and that someone said...

Thankfully, that someone left,
and so I told myself that I
still would not write today
because it would have to be
about that,
and don't you know
that I
want you to think of anything
other than the reason why
I promised myself that I
still would not write today?

It's okay,
it could have been worse.
It's life, but truly,
I might be cursed
for standing there
being perceived as holding back

a story that should have been told
and their history, which never happened.

So, once again,
I promised myself that I
would not write today,
and they were words
that you shouldn't hear,
and it is just life,
and it's just that I should live.

So, for once,
I broke my promise,
grateful I lived.

Better Than the Devil

Add a little of what you know,
sprinkle in a start of what you want,
and stir,
and stir,
until combined.
Better the devil, you know?

As everything else just
slides right by,
and the only reason why
is that this is life,
and this is right,
and this is good,
and some devils do right.
So, better the devil, you know?

Better the devil
who can reach for your past.
Better the devil,
as for them, you will last.
You will stay because
in the duel between devils,
this was the devil
who gave you a taste,
took you into their hands,

and made you a shape,
but you stirred,
and you stirred,
and you held that shape.
That familiar shape
reached and pulled from your past,
and you stayed.
Better the devil, you know?

One day you will see,
deep within that familiar,
that static,
the galaxies that take
shape by your hand,
you
run faster than the devil,
made the most beautiful music,
carried the tree on your back,
and deep in a tired, warm heart
you are found.

I Feel Human

In an instant,
there's some kind of detachment,
and I realize,
I feel less human than I thought I did.

The shapes fit, or at least they used to. For her.
That person they called "her". Restarting the
tangram would allow the realization of what's
missing to appear, but the pieces were never
meant to stay. The scatter is natural.

I feel less human than I thought I did,
and there's a persistant feeling of
attachment.
An unusual answer suggests
depth,
but not to me.
Whispers of the world creep in,
and I feel less human than I thought I did.

When I have an insatiable need for inspiration,
that person they called "her" melts a little bit
more. She doesn't let go because she was a
friend of yours. When I have an insatiable need
for inspiration, I ask in spite of myself. I ask,

and I feel more human than I thought I would be.

Forever or Yesterday

Was it forever ago or yesterday
that the walk went ever on,
and no upward movement was recognized
by the seemingly abandoned road?

Was it forever ago or yesterday
that you noticed the water
to our right,
and you were right?

Was it forever ago or yesterday
that I'd worried too much
over the tip of my shoelace,
and not the walk
that went ever on?

It was once forever ago,
and it was once
a place of their own,
and it was once the walk
they'd walked all those times before.

Yesterday was much the same
in its own way.
Yesterday was buried chains

in other ways.

Yesterday was midnight oil
that became tomorrow's fuel.
Forever, now, is hope.
Tomorrow.
Tomorrow.
Tomorrow.

Perfect

For you, my love,
I'd be a telescope,
and I'd gift you
the universe
as each day
I wake up
and you've
shown me the
universe,
and all I have
are the stars
to return.

You find in this no fault,
you don't see it as less,
and I wonder,
you say you wonder too.

When you gave me the universe,
you held tight to my stars,
so perhaps I am perfect for you.

A Powerful Peace

You feel like retrowave,
like the memories
I will feel tomorrow
and cling to
the next day.

The distance was negligible in the dark room
and closed further with the time spent there. We
aren't the type to take that for granted. I can't
usually open that old chest.

You feel like the midnight hour,
deep in a place that
I call--
I called to
when time was a thing
that could not move.

I had remembered the clouds, the mechanical
nature of what I couldn't decide felt more or less
real. It didn't matter then. This was real, though,
and it was a reality I waited for.

You feel like retrowave,
the kind that fills my mind

and threatens all that moves
past my fingertips
so, so beautifully.

Lacking

I lack control.
I lack structure.
I lack confidence.
I lack assertiveness.
I lack charisma.
I lack energy.
I lack, but I don't,
not really,
only to
fewer
than I can count
on my hand.
I extend my limits.
I extend my power.
I extend it all.
Then, when who I had gained,
saw all I lacked,
they put me in a world where
that is amazing,
and so
I am glad to lack.

Words Enough

To tell you you are beautiful
when words aren't enough
is the feeling
of seeing you smile when
cloth flowers are pressed
in your hand.

To tell you you are kind
when words aren't enough
is to hear you speak
and your heart beat.

To tell you you are funny
when words aren't enough
is to feel happiness come naturally
even when it isn't easy.

To tell you you are love
when words aren't enough
is to know there will never
be words enough.

In Which They Rescue the Princess

Tell me you'll kill a daydream
or that the daydream will melt.
Ice in a bucket.

Then, watch me,
or do not,
build that daydream,
until I live it every day.

Tell me the poison's in my cup,
and take yours.
Watch me,
or do not,
grow and glow
from what would be your poison.

Tell me you'll kill a daydream,
and do not rise with me.
Tell me you'll kill a daydream
or that the daydream will melt.
Ice in a bucket.

The daydream melted
on my tongue

and lived
in my words
which gave hope
to those who would rise with me
and help me live
that daydream.

Treating Rarity

Tell me I'm rare
but close me away
because of the noise
because I am rare,
keep me here,
and bind my hands,
and reach.

Tell me I'm rare,
and allow my ear
to the keyhole.
Didn't you know the door was closed?
Did you see the sun?
Please.

Tell me I'm rare,
but can you not see,
I don't want to be rare.
That's not me.
That's an untouchable being,
some ethereal
fear.

You can reach for me,
expect a new answer,

a change.
It's me, and it's hard to say
that when you tell me I'm rare,
you forget to let me be
one of you.
You forgot you let me be
one of you.

Tell me I'm rare,
and if that image fades,
as it has for me,
the portrait would burn
and the fire would scar.
Do you know that I'm scared
that the fire would scar?

Tell me I'm rare,
and nothing more needs to be said.

The Risks Untaken

If, not if only,
safety was a thing
easily attainable,
it would require
the lifting of a weight
and waiting.

Sometimes, it's easiest to feel safe following a
period of great risk regardless of whether the
outcome is favorable. So much value is attached
to that risk, so when it is over, when it is taken,
safety is what naturally follows.

If, not if only,
surrender to
the strongest forces in the world
created peace and
if, not if only,
the natural result of such a
submission
could then
determine the trajectory of their
sensibilities
or empathy,
then maybe,

some feelings and fears,
only some,
are risks left unclaimed.
Untaken.

The Break

Divert us to an ocean,
at once profound and silent,
and for a while
swim, and allow the waves to
strike, and run away
when it gets too strong.

Keep the rolling action,
the beautifully composed,
and watch it
and read it
and swim in the ocean.

Then.

Then, over and over again,
run away from the wave
and choose the happy ending
and choose the simple,
trope-filled little
something you thought
was a broken promise,
but when you
see beyond the sound,
it wasn't a promise at all.

Just that all-important
break in those
beautiful waves.

It Took Place on an Island I Know

Come to my window
and you do not need to hold
flowers to tell you
the way the petals fall,
but come to my window.
Face my open palm,
and I will reach through.

The space between is not unwelcome, the space
of constant motion. Every important moment
happens here. It constrains, it simplifies. The
space between is a longing to be filled, to satisfy.

3, 2, 1

Come to my window,
and rest on the branch.
Face my open palm
in the manner that
makes me
look away,
but in happiness,
and still desire
to look up again,

and reach.

Sometimes, it takes two.

You Are Not There

You stand in front of her and whisper,
but you are not there.
Her mind stands in front of you,
but though you are not there,
her mind hears the long-forgotten whispers
of the oldest stories ever told.

Told by you, the whisperer,
are the gifts of the past
and their consequences.

You stand in front of her and whisper,
but you are not there.

Told by you, the whisperer,
is all you are
and all you've left,
a quiet cacophony
of what you hope is love,

but you, the whisperer, are not there.

The Seeds

It is time to move
and carry the weight
of intention,
to gather the seeds
and let them fall
as they are intended to.

Seeds are not abandoned
upon their fall from your arms
as they must open their own
to protect their own,
to protect what becomes their own.

Seeds, meant to be scattered to the wind,
uncoil in their beds
with intention
and hope.

When intention bursts forth
from between the rocks,
they became more than themselves.
They curved and curled
and spoke of all they knew of life.

They claim this space.

They cling to light.
They spread their arms
to protect their own.

The Most Powerful Forces

The most powerful forces
in this world are
untouchable,
immovable,
and invisible.

They can touch you,
and that touch can be
sudden.
It can be soft and gentle.
It can be everything,
because they are
the most powerful force in the world.
There, they will remain.

They move by their own force,
creating something like life,
and they do not obey our laws.
There is nothing they cannot move
to or through
because they are
the most powerful force in the world.
There, they can be recognized.

They can appear,

invited or not,
and display the proof
that all that is capable can.

When they take the form of the mountain,
they give the impression of
someone to be held on to,
and in their own way,
they are.

The most powerful forces in this world
build the infinite
and were named
in the only way
we can conceive.

www.ingramcontent.com/pod-product-compliance
Lightning Source LLC
La Vergne TN
LVHW010826200726
843508LV00012B/2512